MW01257828

TURNING THIS THING AROUND

Keith Maginn

Copyright © 2012 Keith Maginn

All rights reserved. No part of this book may be reproduced in any form, by any electronic or mechanical means without permission from the publisher.

DEDICATION

To Grandma Leslie (you are missed) and my parents:
For your example, sacrifices
and unconditional love.

A NOTE FROM THE AUTHOR

One name has been changed in this memoir to protect his/her identity. The rest is completely true.

A NOTE FROM THE AUTHOR

Contents

PART I

HELL

What the hell did we do to deserve this? That question has popped into my head a few dozen times in the past several months. I'm in a shit-hole motel somewhere in Atlanta, but it might as well be a five-star hotel compared to my fiancée's situation: Mary is in a psych ward being treated for severe bipolar/manic depression. I just got off the phone with her. She was hysterical, begging me to sneak her Coca-Cola and muscle-relaxers.

I have no idea what to do or how much longer I can take this. Tears are streaming down my face and I am asking God, once again, for help. My life has fallen apart and I see no daylight ahead.

Mary is still furious with me about check-in night at the "rehabilitation center," as they delicately call it. She is enraged at me because I refused to give her muscle-relaxers despite strict orders to the contrary. Weaning her off the plethora of medications she was on was the whole idea of bringing her here: sixteen prescribed meds daily and another ten to be used "as needed." Up to twenty-six different medications a day for one person (and she weighed less than 120 lbs.)!

And they were not helping; quite the opposite, actually.

I stood firm on that first night, refusing to "help her pain" by disobeying facility commands. Mary cried and told me to leave; she said I must not really love her. I stalled for a few minutes, waiting for her to change her mind. She did not.

Hadn't I proven time after time I would always be there, that I truly loved her and would do anything I could for her? Hadn't I talked her out of suicide multiple times, holding her on the bathroom floor or in bed as she cried uncontrollably night after night? Didn't I lay with her in the hospital telling her things would be better someday? And now she's saying I don't care and she doesn't want me around?

So I left the building.

I went to my car to think for a few minutes. I decided to go back to Mary's room. I asked her if she really wanted me to go. She said if I wouldn't give her the muscle-relaxers, then I should.

I left again.

*

The Most Loving Thing I Could Do

sitting outside your prison
where they're trying to figure you out
wondering why you?
why now?
what's this crazy world all about?

Been trying to read a little
but thinking of you a lot
you're stuck inside alone
wondering if you'll make it or not
I keep tearing up
looking to the sky
drops smack the pavement
as I ask "oh God, why?"

I know you feel so alone
maybe someday it will make sense to you
why I didn't give you what you asked for
that's the most loving thing I could do

I withheld from you
what I was ordered not to give
even when you said
I should leave
there was no reason for you to live
I would give up us

my love
only if that would help you
maybe someday you will understand
that's the most loving thing I could do.

–KM (February '08)

*

Mary had been manic on the drive down from Knoxville, Tennessee, the phase of her illness when she felt indescribable euphoria. I dreaded this stage because of the devastating low that inevitably followed. And it wasn't her; it was a fake happiness, a mirage.

She'd had these sporadic manic periods for years, often staying awake for days. Mary would finish entire novels in one sitting or jog for miles, despite rarely exercising normally. It was a fantasy-like high, as if she were on hallucinogenic drugs.

The rehab center was one highly-monitored hallway of rooms. Patients stood inert with blank expressions on their faces. Others stared at bare walls as if there were no life inside them. I could not tell what gender some of the patients were. There were odd, primal sounds coming out of several rooms.

Nearly all the patients had attempted suicide at least once, some several times. Many were in the midst of electro-shock treatments. It was a sullen, grave place, much like the movie *One Flew Over the Cuckoo's Nest* with Jack Nicholson.

The huge difference to me, of course, was that in this real-life psych ward, my fiancée was the main character.

Mary was adamant that no one know the whole truth of our predicament. A great number of prejudices and stereotypes are associated with mental illness in our society and she did not want to be judged unfairly. Nor did she want pity. My friends and family eventually began to suspect something was not right, but chose not to pry. I admitted to others that Mary struggled with migraines and insomnia—which she did—but no one had a clue how serious her problems were.

In the meantime, I could feel myself slipping away. I was going down with the ship. My mind was a whirlwind of worry, sadness, confusion and anger. It was overwhelming.

I feared I was losing my mind.

Repeatedly, I asked God for help, but things kept getting worse. What did Mary do to deserve this? She was a good person—so great with kids—yet had suffered almost her entire life.

And, what did I do? I was a good person. Had I not spent years in low-paying jobs helping others instead of chasing a bigger paycheck elsewhere? And for what, so we could struggle with bills and barely afford groceries?

I often feared Mary would finally give up. She swore she could never do that to me, but she talked about it often.

We had no idea how long Mary would be at the rehab center. Thank God my boss was understanding and told me to stay as long as I needed and not worry about work right now (I only told my boss that Mary's health was terrible and we were going to a center to help her regulate her medications). I had very little money, hence the shoddy motel. My "smoke-free" room reeked of cigarettes and had multiple burn holes in the drapes and comforter. The cleaning crew neglected to clean the shavings from the previous guest, which were still on the bathroom counter-top and in the sink. Yet compared to Mary's circumstances, I had no right to feel sorry for myself.

After Mary asked me to leave, I drove an hour toward home before I swallowed my pride and returned to be with her. I didn't know if she would pull through. I didn't know if either of us would ever be "okay" again. I had no idea how we'd gotten into this mess or if we could get back out.

Visiting hours at the center were 5 to 9 pm. I spent the days reading and writing, but mostly worrying. I also passed time in a small hospital chapel next door to Mary's facility, meditating and praying. I prayed mostly for Mary, but—for the first time in years—I also prayed for myself.

PART II

BACK TO THE BEGINNING

I suppose my childhood was ordinary for a mid-Western kid. I grew up in the suburbs on the west-side of Cincinnati, the last of four kids. My dad taught at the same school for thirty-one years and coached many of our sports teams while we were growing up. My mom was a homemaker and the PTA president, until we kids were old enough and she went back to school to become an accountant.

I have a lot of respect for my parents for all their hard work and sacrifice. They raised four kids on a teacher's salary, each of us graduating from college. I have never heard them complain. I feel fortunate to have grown up in a stable, loving family. Compared to many, I am lucky.

My brother and two sisters range from two to ten years older than me. All three are successful, happily married and good people. Combined, they have produced eight nieces and nephews that I adore.

Thanks to my brother, his daughter affectionately calls me "Stinky Uncle Keith." My siblings and parents stay busy chasing the kids around and chauffeuring them to practices, plays and so on.

Growing up, the two most important things to me were sports and girls. I can't recall a time in my life when I wasn't infatuated with both. In an effort to keep inquisitive uncles at bay, I did profess to "hate girls" until maybe age thirteen. But, I assure you, this was never the case.

I worked hard in school to get good grades, though teachers sometimes complained I talked too much in class. I have always tried to make people laugh. My late-teen years were uneventful, so I will spare you most of the details: Drinking cheap beer and chasing females became far more important than school, sports or anything else.

I earned a college scholarship and attended Miami University in Oxford, Ohio. I wanted to live away from home, but still be near enough that I could get back to see my family and buddies when I wanted. Miami was a good period for me overall, and I made many good friends to whom I still remain close.

I still had no idea what I wanted to do with my life when I graduated. I did know I wanted to do something altruistic and not work a 9-to-5 job in a dress-shirt and tied to a desk. I thought about joining the Peace Corps, but I was unwilling to be away from my family and friends for such a long time. Somewhere I'd heard about AmeriCorps, a service organization like the Peace Corps, but within the United States. I found a job with AmeriCorps in Knoxville, Tennessee, and moved there a few days after the tragedy of September 11, 2001.

Once in Knoxville, I did two one-year terms for AmeriCorps. AmeriCorps provides workers with a modest "living stipend" to survive on—I believe I made $143 a week my first year and $157 my second—and a $4,725 "education award" upon completion for payment of student loans or for schooling. Though I was paid by AmeriCorps, I worked for Habitat for Humanity, a non-profit organization dedicated to building simple, decent and affordable housing in partnership with those in need, mostly with the help of volunteers. My AmeriCorps service with Habitat was a great experience, and I believe in the Habitat cause enough to be working with them full-time as I write this.

PART III

THE DOWNWARD SPIRAL

-1-

Perhaps much of what I'm writing will come off simply as whining. Your natural inclination might be to think, *Quit crying. My problems are worse than that...*or something similar. After all, we live in a society where no one is ever supposed to complain, and feelings are not to be expressed, especially by males.

So be it.

I am just trying to tell my story and describe my feelings. **In actuality, what got me in much of the mess I finally found myself in was because I kept my mouth shut and suffered in silence for years.** Kay Redfield Jamison says in the national bestseller *An Unquiet Mind: A Memoir of Moods and Madness,* "It was a costly attitude; [my] upbringing and pride held [me] hostage."

Always at my inner core—though very minute at

low points in my life—has been a belief that every-thing happens for a reason. Someday I would be glad that I've been through what I have.

I believe that now more than ever. I've learned how fragile people are and how important we are to each other.

Things are looking up for me, but not too long ago my world was falling apart and my mind was spiral-ing out-of-control. I want to tell you what helped me turn things around. But, first, I need to tell you about the darkness that enveloped me before I finally saw some daylight.

By all outward appearances, I was a happy, fun-loving guy growing up, going to college and finding my way to Knoxville. Not even my family or closest friends knew anything was wrong. They only saw the public face I put on, always laughing and having a good time.

Perhaps I should have pursued an acting career, because on the inside I was quite the opposite: I was bitter and confused. I was in pain every day and felt sleepy nearly all the time. I can't pinpoint when my back began bothering me or when I started feeling chronically tired, but I also can't recall a time in my life when I wasn't this way. If I had to guess, I'd say the back pain came on in my early teens and the daily fatigue pre-dated even that. Was there a time when I wasn't struggling to stay awake every time I slowed down for a few minutes?

But it was just how I was; I didn't know anything else. I *did* know that it's not good to complain—everyone has problems—so it was grin and bear it. This is the message we get in our society: *Suck it up...Walk it off*....Only my immediate family was aware I had any health problems, and just that my back bothered me at times.

My lower-back pain continued to get worse throughout college. I never had any energy and took naps as much as possible. I attributed my weariness to late hours of studying or drinking with friends until the sun came up.

But despite getting to bed at a more reasonable time and cutting back on the partying after I graduated, things did not improve. Getting out of bed was a challenge every morning, as I felt like I hadn't slept at all. Naturally, since back pain woke me several times each night, I thought all of my problems were related to my back pain.

In January of 2002, after years of living with the discomfort, I finally decided no one should have to live in pain every day, especially an otherwise fit person in their early 20s. I looked around at my peers and saw many who didn't exercise, that smoked, ate junk and fast-food regularly and yet seemed to feel good. With the exception of drinking too much beer, I was doing everything right, but still felt miserable every day. I thought this was very unfair and the bitterness continued growing inside me.

My first attempt at relief was to see a chiropractor. I went a few times a week for several weeks, but to no avail. The final straw was when the doctor brought out before/after X-rays to show my progress. He raved about how much better my spine looked—*despite the obvious fact that I did not feel any better.*

But there was something else: There were distinct vertical zippers on the hip pockets that showed up on the "new and improved" X-ray. Now, as a child of the 80s, I liked Michael Jackson as much as the next kid. But I wasn't still wearing the multi-pocketed parachute pants in my early-20s! I didn't own pants that had zippers on the pockets and this was obviously not me.

After much embarrassment and many apologies on the chiropractor's part, I decided to try a different route. I gave acupuncture an honest try for several weeks and found it interesting. But, again, no luck.

Next, my primary-care physician sent me to a rheumatologist to treat me for suspected arthritis. I underwent numerous tests, more X-rays (no zippers magically appeared this time!), bone scans and MRIs. I tried all kinds of drugs. Still, nothing touched the pain.

Despite not having a remedy, three rheumatologists diagnosed me as having "ankylosing spondylitis," a chronic inflammatory disease. AS is an arthritic disease of the inactive form, meaning the longer I am inert, the worse it gets. Therefore, it is most painful after being in bed a few hours and gets better throughout the day. It is a dull, nagging pain and mundane everyday things like getting out of bed, tying my shoes and sneezing can be painful.

Though happy to have a diagnosis, I was still at a loss. It was terribly frustrating to go from a check-up once a year ("I don't need to go the doctor!") to seeing several doctors dozens of times a year. And still no relief.

Every doctor I saw eventually shrugged and said they didn't have an answer. I was "an enigma" and was left with: "Sometimes chronic pain is just something some people have to live with, your cross to bear so to speak." They also informed me that in extreme cases, people with AS can become hunchbacks by the age of 35: not what someone wants to hear, especially a seemingly fit male in his early 20s that hopes to live a long life.

But there was no way I was going to accept this diagnosis and resign myself to a life of misery. I continued to go on endless numbers of doctor visits and had every test imaginable done to me. Hurry up and wait, over and over again.

During this period, I went from not owning a credit card to being a few thousand dollars in debt. All-in-all, I went to well over a hundred appointments and spent several thousand dollars and yet I still felt the same: pain every night and day. I tried to stay optimistic, but it seemed to be one disappointment after another.

If this wasn't frustrating enough—pain and fatigue daily for years, sickening amounts of tests and doctor visits, and extreme financial stress—I had to find a new career. Service in AmeriCorps was limited to two one-year terms, so I needed to think about my future. I'd decided to pursue a career in firefighting.

While working full-time at Habitat on weekdays, I graduated from a local firefighter academy that met at night and on weekends. I often put in 70-plus hours a week. When my time with AmeriCorps was up, I worked exclusively with the fire department, pulling a few 24-hour shifts a week.

Being a fireman seemed like the perfect career for me: I would be helping people in an exciting, ever-changing job that was physically demanding; not to mention that I would have a good deal of down-time to read, write and exercise. But, after two years of hard work and sacrifice, I had to admit that it was not going to work out. The back pain was bad enough, but the chronic fatigue really worried me:

Would I be alert enough to perform at my best in extremely serious circumstances?

I knew the answer was no. I broke the news to my Lieutenant and my firefighter buddies and went in search of something new. I looked and looked, but found nothing. I applied to all kinds of jobs, but once again I had no idea what I wanted to do. I'd finally found a meaningful career, but I had to abandon that path due to health issues.

After the doctors shrugged and sent me on my way with "my cross to bear," I tried another route. I suspected something else entirely might be causing my chronic fatigue. During the day, I'd fight falling asleep at my desk. I even began nodding off while driving to work in the morning. No matter how much sleep I got, every morning it felt like I hadn't slept at all.

Not a good way to start the day. Every single day.

My physician directed me to undergo testing at a sleep study center. At the center, I was shown to a small suite, much like a hotel room. At bedtime, a nurse began attaching stuff all over my body: wires down my T-shirt stuck to my chest, others down my shorts and attached to my legs and still more stuck to my head.

The nurse told me to lie down—"make yourself comfortable"—with a video-camera staring down at me. I'm thinking, *oh God, what if I play with myself during the night*? Sorry, but I am a guy; we do this sometimes without knowing it. I look like Franken-stein-in-his-pajamas, I'm on video surveillance by complete strangers and I am worried that I might wake up in the morning with an erection.

And I fall asleep in less than one minute.

My results showed a sleep disorder called sleep apnea in which breathing repeatedly stops and starts throughout sleep. Sleep apnea, wasn't that something only overweight middle-aged men have, as in very big guys that shake the house with their snoring? But I was a slim, 165 pound guy in my mid-20s.

What?

My sleep study indicated that my breathing stops several times each hour, which obviously disrupts the sleep cycle and causes excessive daytime sleepiness. My prize was to sleep with a CPAP mask every night, a Darth Vader-like contraption strapped to my face so that air could blow in my mouth to keep my airway open. I gave it my best shot, thinking, *I can tolerate this if it finally helps me feel rested in the morning.* But after months of trying, I couldn't get used to the thing at all.

The doctors at the sleep center then wanted me to ask my dentist about making an apparatus to help my sleep apnea. It was a special mouthpiece that would better open my airway. My dentist agreed to make it, but my health insurance provider nixed the idea: Since the apparatus would be made by a dentist, they wouldn't cover it. This despite the fact it was for a medical condition for which I had 100 percent coverage. It would cost me several hundred dollars out-of-pocket, so it was not an option.

Next, I saw an Ear, Nose and Throat doctor, who informed me I have a deviated septum in my nose that blocks a good deal of my airway in my left nostril. A lot of blood, discomfort and a thousand dollar surgery later, and I didn't feel any improvement at all.

So now what?

While I struggled with my health and looked for a new career, my girlfriend of nearly six years left me.

We had met in Panama Beach, where both of us were vacationing with friends. She was from a small town—when I say small, I mean tiny—in west Tennessee and had the sweetest Southern accent I had ever heard. We were both immediately "smitten" (her term, which made me melt) and kept in touch when we both returned home.

Despite the distance between us, we got serious and fell in love. We wrote long love letters and poems to each other, talked or e-mailed nearly every day and took turns visiting the other at our respective colleges. It was like a fairy tale.

For about four years, we kept up this long-distance relationship. After I got a job in Knoxville, she moved across the state to be with me. We were in love and I assumed we would get married someday soon. She was my best friend and knew me better than anyone ever had.

In retrospect, we had our problems and I'm sure I wasn't always a joy to be around. She saw my health issues and my job situation firsthand. I was trying hard to pull out of my rut. I felt I would get a break soon and everything would be good again.

I thought it was something we would get through together.

I was wrong.

Without warning, she told me it was over. I was shocked and deeply hurt. I couldn't believe that she would leave me when I needed her most.

But, looking back, I can't really blame her.

I was single once again, confused and heartbroken. I didn't know what to do. I dreaded going to work and was barely scraping by. After my long-time love left, I finally found a 30-hour-a-week job—without medical benefits—at a small college library in town. Hardly my dream job, but it was the best thing I could find at the time. I was struggling, but doing everything I could to stay afloat.

I was so sick of being exhausted, in pain and without any answers. I became depressed and all I wanted to do was stay in bed. I kept going to work and the gym and occasionally got together with friends, but mostly I just wanted to be alone.

Then, out-of-the-blue, my former boss at Habitat for Humanity called and said a position had opened up. It was terribly low-paying, but it was a full-time job with an organization I believed in. Most importantly, it included medical benefits.

I accepted the job, delighted with my stroke of good fortune. Maybe things were finally starting to look up. Was my luck finally going to change?

And then I met Mary.

I had been single for nearly two years. After persistent pestering from a friend, I swallowed my pride and checked out the on-line dating world. I wasn't too optimistic about the whole thing, but eventually I connected with an attractive young lady that seemed fun and unique. A few introductory e-mails were followed by some marathon phone sessions; we hit it off right away and decided to meet in person.

She lived "in the condo with the fiesta lights on all year" and would prove to be every bit the free-spirit I had expected. I was extremely nervous as she opened the door; she later told me my shyness was "so cute." I was floored when I first saw Mary in person. She was absolutely drop-dead.

My first thought was, *Wow, she is way out-of-my-league* (which tells you not only how beautiful she was, but also about my self-esteem). I brought presents for Mary's beloved cat, which went over well with pet and owner. We drank some wine (Mary and me, not the cat) and picked up our conversation again like we'd known each other for years.

The two of us connected so fast that it seemed like something out of a movie. We eventually went out for a late Mexican dinner and everything went perfectly. The whole night seemed magical, surreal.

I vividly recall waking up the next morning thinking my life had changed literally overnight. Mary told me she felt the same. We fell fast and hard. The two of us spent every non-working moment together and, at Mary's insistence, I moved in with her after only a month of dating. After all, she reasoned, we were together all the time; why not share an apartment and cut our rent in half?

Mary seemed to glow and her friends and family said they had never seen her so healthy and happy. I felt like I was walking on air. Meeting Mary had completely turned my life around.

Almost instantly, we had fallen in love. Everything was amazing. I'd never felt that way in my life and each day was new and exciting. I often found myself smiling for no apparent reason.

Both of us were the happiest we had ever been in our lives.

Then the rug was yanked out from beneath us.

Mary told me early on that she suffered from bi-polar/manic depression, but she said her medications were helping a lot and she was doing great. She was so happy and carefree. Things were going so well that I didn't think much about it.

When I met Mary, she was working with kids in a variety of occupations, which always made her full of life. Mary was good with kids. She was also hard-working, putting in 60 or more hours a week. I loved these two qualities about her.

But a few weeks after I moved in, Mary was unable to work at all. She spent most of her time in bed or in the bathtub. This went on for months.

About two months after we met, Mary got a staph infection from one of the kids she cared for. The meds that had been helping her depression were overpowered by the new ones for treating the infection. It was literally like someone flipped a light switch, a complete 180.

Mary's depression was dumb-founding. She went from the most free-spirited, fun person I'd ever met to the most self-loathing, sad person I had ever seen. By far. She spent countless hours crying in bed. It was heartbreaking. Manic depression is a horrible mental illness and I would not wish that kind of pain on anyone.

Making matters worse, Mary had crippling migraines and suffered from insomnia, often going days without sleep. She was also hypoglycemic (low blood sugar, which sometimes made her faint) and had a painful tumor in her foot the size of a golf ball. She had suffered with these multiple ailments for years. I could not believe how much one person had to deal with.

I found it hard to accept that I could not help Mary. All I could do was keep loving her and trying to support her. But nothing I did seemed to help whatsoever.

*

How can I make happy the sad girl
Sitting in the rain
Waiting
Laying in bed
No sleep
What do you do
When nothing you do's enough
Will you ever be
How can I make happy
The sad girl
How can I reflect her

From my eyes
How can I bring light
To her world
How can I put sunshine
In her skies

Here comes the rain again
Mixing in with the tears
Is there a way to show you care
A way to end her fears

How can I convince her
Can I ever make her see
I'm not going anywhere
But she's running away from me

How can I make happy
The sad girl
How can I reflect her
From my eyes
How can I bring light
To her world
How can I put sunshine
In her skies

–KM (June '07)

*

Looking back, I can honestly say I did everything I could possibly do for Mary. I was dangerously close to losing my sanity in the process. I tried to help Mary's self-esteem often in what I said and in poems and little notes I would leave around the house. But she was convinced that she was not special, beautiful or intelligent, though she was all of these; no matter how many times I said it, Mary didn't believe me.

She turned heads everywhere we went and yet somehow thought herself hideous. Her self-loathing was mind-boggling. Kay Redfield Jamison, an expert in manic depression (and herself a manic-depressive), says in *An Unquiet Mind*: "No amount of love can cure madness or unblacken one's dark moods. Love can help, it can make the pain more tolerable, but, always, one is beholden to medication that may or may not always work and may or may not be bearable."

I was by her side as much as I possibly could be. I sincerely loved Mary and was willing to do anything I could for her. She often told me I was the only thing keeping her alive.

Not that I am claiming to be a saint by any means.

My own problems were all I could handle and now the person I loved was falling apart. The bitterness inside me was eating me up. I was angry at the world—angry at God—so I'm sure I was not always pleasant to be around. I tried to shield her from my issues, but it was sometimes too much for me. My family, friends and co-workers didn't see my hidden anger, but Mary saw it.

Mary and I had incredibly touching moments together. A large part of our strong bond was a shared compassion for all the other was going through. We understood better than most what the other endured. I realized she was sad and discouraged; she knew I was furious and confused. We both were aware we had done nothing to deserve these hands we'd been dealt and that we were doing everything we possibly could.

*

two sad souls
trying to find
happiness
together

−KM (June '07)

*

But we sometimes had explosive arguments. Mary seemed to be able to turn nearly everything I said into something somehow against her. I'd compliment her dress and she'd claim I was just saying that to be nice and I probably thought she was ugly. "Why was I even with her?" she'd ask. As her therapists pointed out many times, she frequently pushed people away, testing them to see if they'd come back to her (For example, the night she ordered me to leave the rehab center.).

I was at my wit's end and my anger sometimes exploded. In retrospect, I did the best I could in drastic conditions, but I can't say I am proud of how I acted 100 percent of the time. I remember a lot of door slamming by both of us during this time. I even punched a wall once (which I thought was dry-wall and turned out to be cement; served me right).

Somehow I kept a happy-on-the-surface demeanor at work and in public. Only a few close friends later told me they'd begun to suspect something was wrong, but they never asked. I probably would have shrugged them off if they had. I snuck into the bathroom at work a few times to burst into tears without anyone noticing. As I wrote back then: "I have to leave early for work these days/just in case I break down."

Although not even close to Mary's problems, I had about all I could handle of my own difficulties. Chronic pain and fatigue daily, extreme financial concerns and now, I had to admit, full-blown depression. Starting off every day in pain and feeling like you didn't sleep a bit is no way to go through life.

But to see the person you love suffer far more, to the extent that they no longer want to live, was too much for me. I knew I was sinking mentally, like a slow descent in quicksand: The more I struggled to get out, the deeper I sank. I didn't know if I'd be able to get back to solid ground.

*

I wish I knew you when you were
a little girl
I wish I was there to catch your first tear
I wish I was your first dance, first kiss,
first love
I wish we'd watched the clouds together
as kids and dreamed
I wish we still had that childlike innocence,
spontaneity and fun
I wish I was there for you every time
you were sad
I wish I was enough
I wish I made you happy
I wish you could be happy
I wish I could be happy
I wish we could be happy

−KM (December '07)

*

Though I did my best to put on a happy public face, inside I was increasingly bitter. I could not help but think how unfair all this was. Life was little more than a struggle every single day for years. Naïvely, I thought I'd somehow be rewarded for my altruism and sacrifice; instead I felt cursed. And the young woman I loved had issues far worse than mine. How could God let this happen?

It was all I could do to make it to work every day. Looking back, I really don't know how I went in, acting like nothing was wrong, except that I had no other choice. I would have taken several weeks off, but that was not an option: We needed my paycheck desperately and I was dependent on my medical benefits.

I would head home from work every evening not knowing if we would be going to the emergency room that night, if Mary would be in bed knocked out by meds for a migraine or if she would be curled up on the bathroom floor sobbing for hours. The stress was unbearable. It overcame me one night, as my thoughts raced out-of-control.

Driving home alone, I had to pull to the side of the highway. I was seconds away from calling 911 before I regained my wits. It is a scary feeling when your worry takes over and you cannot control your thoughts.

I finally decided I had to see a therapist. I felt I had no other alternatives. I didn't know how much more I could take and expected any day I'd have a nervous breakdown. I worried I might be losing my mind.

I couldn't betray Mary's trust and let others know

what was really going on. I also didn't want to burden anybody with my problems either. Therefore, the only person I could talk to was a therapist. As I wrote in my journal: "...and so I have to pay someone to listen to me because no one wants to hear me complain and I don't want my problems to be known or become theirs."

I felt stuck in an elaborate maze with only dead-ends. The person I wanted to turn to, Mary, was far too wrapped up in her own nightmare to be able to help me. When this happens, the anger has nowhere to go but inside you. That is what depression is: anger turned inward.

*

i walk around
It appears i am alive
only i know
i am dead inside

−KM (April '08)

During this extremely turbulent time, Mary believed that the two of us getting engaged would "make everything better." It would "prove that I really loved her—even at her absolute worst—and make her so happy." I loved Mary and wanted to be engaged some day, but I knew this was not the right time.

Nor was it the solution to her problems.

However, eventually I gave in to Mary's persistence, and I asked her to marry me. On her birthday, I dropped to one knee at the restaurant where we had our first date (Embarrassingly, I couldn't afford a decent ring, so she had picked out a "for now" ring on Overstock.com for less than $150.). However unhealthy we were, I loved Mary and felt I was doing this for her happiness and to preserve her delicate mental state.

And it did actually help.

For a few days.

Meanwhile, my now-fiancée continued to get worse. One night, out-of-nowhere, she told me she was pregnant. This news shocked me because Mary always swore that she took her birth control religiously. She'd always loved kids and thought kids of her own would "finally make her happy some day." But we'd agreed now was definitely not the time to have a child together.

I could only wonder...

I was worried because Mary was a walking pharmacy of potent drugs and it didn't take a PhD to realize how bad that could be for an unborn child. She had nightmares that she would lose the baby.

This would soon prove true.

Mary was devastated and it sent her still deeper into her abyss. I did not know if she would ever be able to pull herself out.

I provided as much support for Mary as I could. It was terrible seeing her suffer so much. But, I admit, I thought the miscarriage was a blessing from God. There was no way the two of us could raise a child. We were not stable, functioning adults able to provide for

a newborn. We were struggling in every way con-
ceivable: physically, emotionally, spiritually and fi-
nancially. And who knew if the baby would have
been able to survive if he/she were severely dam-
aged by exposure to toxic chemicals?

*

For Mary
I find myself crying
Every day now
Some for me
Mostly for you
Knowing there's been pain
In every single day
You've made it thru
So many have left your side
Along the way
But I promise you
I won't
Just because
You can't see
How beautiful
How special you are
Doesn't mean
I don't

–KM (November '07)

*

I could not believe trained doctors could allow one person to be on so many drugs at once. Many of them counteracted one another and caused horrible side effects. The drugs interacted dangerously and unpredictably. Mary eventually developed a painful uterine disease that doctors attributed to years of putting so many powerful narcotics in her body. They believed the disease would bother her for the rest of her life.

Mary's overmedication and deepening depression took us to Atlanta and the horror that awaited us.

11

After the rehab staff in Atlanta worked with Mary's medications for four exceptionally emotional and stressful days, not much changed. We returned to Knoxville and tried to move forward, but it was more of the same. Tense and desperate are the best words I can use, though they don't fully do the situation justice. Despite all my efforts, I could not argue that Mary had sunk to a critical low.

We may never know how much those drugs did to help Mary, but it all seemed extremely unsafe to me. Elizabeth Gilbert, courageously discussing her own depression in *Eat, Pray, Love*:

> I do know these drugs made my misery feel less catastrophic. So I'm grateful for that. But I'm still deeply ambivalent about mood-altering medications. I'm awed by their power, but concerned by their prevalence. I think they need to be prescribed and used with much more restraint in this country, and never without the parallel treatment of psychological counseling. Medicating the symptom of any illness without exploring its root cause is

just a classically hare-brained Western way to think that anyone could ever truly get better. Those pills might have saved my life, but they did so only in conjunction with about twenty other efforts I was making simultaneously during that same period to rescue myself, and I hope to never have to take such drugs again.

Seemingly out-of-the-blue, Mary began talking one night about moving to Ireland. She wanted to get away from her life here and asked if I would go with her, to start over. Could this get any crazier?

I told Mary I did not see how this plan was possible. We had no money and I desperately needed my health insurance. Where would we live? Where would I work? We couldn't even afford plane tickets.

I also told Mary, as gently as I could, that her problems would still be there no matter where she went. Moving somewhere new might help for a short period, but the demons were inside her and as such would follow her anywhere. I tried to provide reason to what I saw as a drastic and futile plan.

Despite my protests, Mary decided to go. Alone. Almost immediately, she found a job listed online as a nanny for a family in Ireland. She would be gone for three weeks, a month at the most.

I wrote her a poem the night before she was to leave:

We started off together
Hopeful
Naïve
Side-by-side
Always
We'd never want to leave
So many hopes
Dreams
Love without care
We swore whatever happened
That is what we'll share

Then somewhere
Somehow
Our worlds fell apart
We show each other anger
Sadness
In our hearts
But don't you know
My love
Though overtaken
By despair
If that is what we're given
That is what we'll share

We can get thru this hell
But only side-by-side
When we remember the love we have

Not the pain we hold inside
You've had so much
In life to go through
But don't you know
I'm in pain, too
All I want is us
Both parts
Of an inseparable pair
When we become closer
Stronger
That is what we'll share

Time goes by
We continue
To grow
You see my love
Daily
A love
only you know
When the time comes
One is called
up there
We will wait
Patiently
To be reunited
*And **that is what we'll share***

—KM (March '08)

But this trip to Ireland was something she had to do. So she left.

-12-

you left me to find yourself
not for another
but when you went away
you took all my color

–KM (April '08)

Despite promising to contact me immediately up-on her arrival in Ireland so that I knew she was safe, I heard nothing. A few days passed. A week went by. Then two weeks. Was she okay? Had something ter-rible happened? Had she given up on us? How could Mary put me through this anxiety?

I couldn't do anything except wait and worry.

Finally, after almost three weeks I got an e-mail: She was sorry she hadn't contacted me, but she hadn't known what to say. Mary said she loved me, but she was happy in Ireland. She went on to apolo-gize for messing up my life and said she just wanted me to be happy.

I was devastated and confused. I had no thought of giving up on Mary and every intention of seeing this through to what I thought could quite possibly be a tragic end for one or both of us. I had slipped down mentally to the most depressed I had ever been and I could not fathom it could get any worse. I had kept her alive and done everything I possibly could and that was it?

There had been times in the early going when Mary had said that she wished she were stronger and could break things off with me, because she loved me and didn't want me to suffer. She "felt so guilty for ruining my life." I didn't know if she were cutting ties with me out of love—essentially to save me—or because she instinctively knew she could only get through this on her own. Maybe it was a last-ditch effort, forcing her to sink or swim to save herself.

I may never know.

I haven't seen her since.

13

I did not want to get out of bed, let alone leave my apartment. I didn't want to see anyone, except for Mary. I had prayed to God for help many times and it seemed to fall on deaf ears, only to get worse and worse. I was in debt, alone, broken-hearted, deeply depressed, exhausted and angry to my core.

I did the only thing I knew to do: I cried out.

I finally turned to my family and friends. Looking back, I am 100 percent convinced that it was the only thing I could do to keep me from going over the edge. I was in the deepest abyss of my life and I had little will-to-live.

I called my parents and told them the whole truth about what had been going on. I felt useless and used, angry and sad. I told them about Mary leaving for Ireland, about my depression and that I was in therapy. I felt horrible upsetting them with my whole truth, but it was all I knew to do.

I told my parents I believed that I had always been depressed, even as a little boy. My goofing around and laughing was a cover for my inner sadness. I felt my level of happiness was usually a little below average to far below average, whatever "average" may be. But it was rarely good. And currently it was dangerously low.

Sure I had good times, but they were the exception. The events of the past ten months or so had simply brought my sadness more to the surface. My mom was shocked: "But you were always laughing and joking around, the life of the party." I replied, "I thought everyone knew that clowns and comedians are often the saddest people in the world."

I would say that night was the lowest point of my life, the most depressed I've ever been. When I got off the phone, I fell down on the floor sobbing, clutching my hair with both hands. I got a splitting headache and all I wanted to do was sleep. I was tired of the pain, worry and sadness. I felt like I was in handcuffs and had no idea where to find the key. I asked God why I had to suffer so much.

The next day I sent an e-mail to my family and close friends. With Mary gone, I no longer had to hold this nightmare inside. I *could no longer* hold it inside. I told them everything: Mary's severe depression and the miscarriage, her move to Ireland, my own depression and therapy.

And, again, I am certain that doing that—and the resultant support—probably saved my life.

14

I was beginning, but *just* beginning, to understand that not only my mind but also my life was at stake. I had not been brought up to submit without a fight, however. I really believed all of the things I had been taught about weathering it through, self-reliance, and not imposing your problems on other people. But looking back over the wreckage brought about by this kind of blind stupidity and pride, I now wonder, What on earth could I have been thinking? I also had been taught to think for myself: Why, then, didn't I question these rigid, irrelevant notions of self-reliance? Why didn't I see how absurd my defiance really was?

–Kay Redfield Jamison, *An Unquiet Mind*

The support from my loved ones was amazing. Family members offered to drive down to Knoxville from Cincinnati. Friends told me I could move in with them and start over. Many called or e-mailed almost immediately and others sent cards: "You are special, don't forget that...you will get through this and be better for it...things will get better, hang in there... we're praying for you and we love you...everything happens for a reason...."

I needed every bit of it.

If there had been a silver lining, it was that I learned a valuable lesson about love and friendship. I am forever in debt to everyone that stepped up in my time of need. I honestly don't know what I would have done without them.

I saved all the e-mails from loved ones at that time and was amazed recently when I read my replies: As low as I was, I kept saying things like "this might be a blessing in disguise" and "maybe someday I will be glad this happened." This told me that **at my lowest point, I still had a little faith.**

That's about all I had.

PART IV

TURNING THIS THING AROUND

-1-
Out of the darkness

"I'm not what I ought to be,
I'm not what I'm going to be,
but thank God I'm not what I used to be."

-_____

It has been more than eighteen months since Mary left for Ireland. By no means do I claim to be 100 percent "healed" or "whole." I am still working on that. I have good days and bad days. I have come a long way, but I have a long way still to go.

I am no self-help guru. In fact, I do not claim to be an expert in anything. I know many people have made it through far worse times than I have encountered, and I do not claim to have had the most difficult life whatsoever. But I do know I was pushed to my own absolute limit and thought I might never recover. I have been so far down that I could think of little reason to keep living.

Self-help experts, doctors and the like can certainly provide support and have a lot to offer, but unless they've been there themselves, how much can they really know? In the words of Kay Redfield Jamison in *An Unquiet Mind*: "But, as I well knew, an understanding at an abstract level does not necessarily translate into an understanding at a day-to-day level. I have become fundamentally and deeply skeptical that anyone who does not have this illness can truly understand it."

I have read more than my share of self-help books that claim these ten steps will do this, these eighteen rules will do that and the one-hundred-and-one things you must do today in order to be perfect tomorrow. I think you know what I mean. Enough already!

I am not going to give you a set number of "steps" or "rules" to do anything; I'm simply going to tell you what has helped me. In doing so, I hope you might benefit as well. Even if you only get one thing out of this, at least we've made some progress together. After all, there's got to be a reason why I felt I had to write this book, just as there's a reason why you are reading it.

Again, I realize I have a long way to go in my own life. I have my issues, my shortcomings. But I feel I am finally finding my path. Maybe by telling you what has helped me turn things around for myself, it might help you or a loved one in some way. It has been a long, difficult process, but the sun is shining again.

Facing my demons

Ever since I was a boy, I was terribly self-conscious and super-sensitive. Some of my earliest memories—I must have been about five years old—are of being at my local swim-club in the summer-time. Older kids and adults frequently commented on how skinny I was, which made me very insecure when I was shirtless at swim lessons. I would cross my arms in front of me, acting like I was cold, to hide my scrawny body.

I also had acne and felt my skin looked horrible to everyone who saw me. Unless you have had acne yourself, it is hard to understand how greatly it can affect your self-confidence and self-esteem.

Despite my objections, my parents put me in braces as a teenager, and I am not referring to the hardly noticeable kind they make nowadays: I mean the huge-metallic-train track-looking-bear-traps that came equipped with rubber-bands. Seems almost funny now, but at the time it made my sense of worth even worse. There were many times that I avoided people and social settings because of my self-consciousness.

As I said earlier, I was also the last of four kids. I don't know if it was real or imagined, but I always tried to live up to some standard of excellence. My sisters were both exceptional students and my brother a star athlete. To keep up, I strove to be outstanding in the classroom and in sports.

I often played the class clown seeking attention and looking for approval outside myself. I never really understood it, but I was always popular with the other kids—males and, more importantly, females. For the most part I kept my insecurities effectively hidden to the outside world. My closest friends had no idea that I was actually shy by nature and extremely self-conscious. I had a lot of friends and, in an effort to hide my discomfort from others, acted like the life of the party.

But I was painfully aware of the truth.

By the time I got to college, something started to change. I began having problems with blushing. It may not sound like much, but it is a very uncomfortable experience. It's a vicious cycle: You feel yourself blushing, which makes you still more embarrassed and you blush even more. As John R. Marshall, M.D. says in *Social Phobia*: "I have always considered it a cruel twist of fate when people who already dread and suffer under the scrutiny of others must undergo the added fear or the outright embarrassment of blushing—a betrayal of their deepest, most secret responses to the world they fear spread across their faces for all to see."

I deftly avoided any classes in which I would have to do any oral presentation whatsoever. I would ask around, researching each possible class to make sure I would not be put in the position of having to give a speech. I was absolutely terrified of public speaking.

It didn't matter if I were speaking in front of three people or fifty, complete strangers or good friends. For example, I once had to do a short presentation for a kindergarten class when I worked for the fire department. I was horrified. This is quite embarrassing to share, but it's the truth. Something in me was scared-to-death.

Comedian Jerry Seinfeld once said that public speaking is people's number one fear, even ahead of death. He points out that people would rather be in the casket at a funeral than giving the eulogy. Funny, I agree, but there is some truth in this for me.

There was one college class I could not get out of that required an oral presentation: *Introduction to Sociology*. It was a fairly large class, maybe fifty to seventy-five students. As I sat in the back row and was one of the last to get the sign-up sheet, I got stuck with a date for my speech well into the semester. I dreaded that day with a passion and stressed over it for weeks.

Judgment Day finally arrived and I did the best I

could. I was so nervous that I could hear my voice shaking, like I was standing on a vibrating platform. It was humiliating.

I soldiered through the best I could, but I was certain I'd made a fool of myself. It didn't help that the best looking girl at Miami was in this class (needless to say, I never asked her out).

After this nightmare, I sought help. I saw a therapist for the first time in my life and was diagnosed with "social anxiety disorder" (a.k.a. "social phobia"). The Mayo Clinic's Web site (www.mayoclinic.com) defines social anxiety disorder as "a chronic mental health condition that causes an irrational anxiety or fear of activities or situations in which you believe that others are watching you or judging you."

Social anxiety disorder is beyond just being shy and affects the quality of life of its prisoners. For example, many people might be a little uncomfortable introducing themselves to the class on the first day of school. But for people like me, it's something we lose sleep over for days in advance.

As the Mayo Clinic explains, social anxiety disorder poses unique difficulties:

> When you have social anxiety disorder, you realize that your anxiety or fear is out of proportion to the situation. Yet you're so worried about developing social anxiety dis-

order symptoms that you avoid situations that may trigger them. And indeed, just worrying about having any symptoms can cause them.

I was given medication, which I tried for some time. However, it didn't seem to help and I gave up on the idea for the time being. I hoped I'd grow out of it or confront it at another time. I continued to avoid any embarrassing situations the best I could. But my social anxiety persisted, sometimes lurking quietly in the background and other times loud and out-in-the-open.

Again, I believe I appeared "normal" to most people, but I was in turmoil on the inside. "There is often a big gap between outward appearances and inner reality," says the Dalai Lama.

*

As I write this book, I am proud to say that I am finally confronting my biggest fear. After years of avoidance, I have finally gotten up the courage to face my social anxiety head-on. Deep down, I always knew I would have to deal with it; it was not something that would go away on its own.

When I was struggling with the Mary situation, my primary physician suggested I see a psychiatrist for anti-depressant medication and a psychologist for therapy. I was able to make an appointment with Joey Parker, a Psychiatric Nurse Practitioner. I found him to be an intelligent, friendly guy, probably not much older than me. I tried several medications, but we couldn't find the right one for me.

One crucial thing Joey did was recommend a psychologist, Dr. Keith Hulse. Joey had said the health professionals going to therapy that he knew went to Dr. Hulse, which I considered good counsel. I would soon find out that his good reputation was well-deserved.

I've been extremely fortunate to have a good therapist on my side. Dr. Hulse has helped me quite a bit with all of my issues and especially with my social anxiety. He has worked patiently with me, allowing me to work at my own pace.

When the frequency of my blushing continued to increase, Dr. Hulse encouraged me to go back to Joey Parker. I'd started blushing more than ever: During meetings at work, chance encounters at the grocery store with people I knew and so on.

Joey had me try a new medication, which to my pleasant surprise has helped my blushing a lot. It is so comforting not to have to worry about my face turning red in front of others, blatantly signaling my awkwardness.

With my blushing much more under control, Dr.

Hulse and I began to work on my social anxiety. His plan was to put me in situations that would trigger my anxiety, so that I could learn to overcome it (the technical term is "In Vivo Desensitization"). We made a list of situations that would produce fear in me, starting basic and progressing to more nerve-racking conditions. The idea, obviously, is to build up my self-confidence as I exposed myself more to what produced nervousness. His example: "If you are learning how to swim, you don't just jump straight into the deep end."

My first "homework assignment" was to increase the times I initiated interactions in public. I was to greet more strangers, ask more questions and so on. This was relatively easy for me, but I understood the process: Baby steps.

Dr. Hulse had often encouraged me to join a club/group/team of some sort, to be around new people, as I usually surrounded myself in a safe co-coon of friends and people I was comfortable with. This would be my next step. With some trepidation, I started going to yoga classes and it has been a rewarding experience. I have greatly enjoyed the classes, as well as meeting new people.

The homework then called for me to give speeches in front of a mirror. I did not think this would be difficult at all, but it actually caused me a surprising amount of anxiety initially. With frequent practice, my anxiety abated. (I gave speeches in my bathroom with the exhaust fan running, so my neighbors upstairs couldn't hear me talking to myself night after night.)

Next, I was to continue with the speeches, but now voice-record them also (ideally, we would have used a video-camera, but I didn't have access to one). I expected this would raise my anxiety somewhat, but it did not. However, I knew the tough stuff was approaching fast.

Early in the process, Dr. Hulse asked how I would feel giving speeches to him at some point. Immediately, I could feel the anxiety and blood rushing to my head. I didn't understand it: Here was a person I liked and was comfortable with. I'd worked with him dozens of times and Dr. Hulse probably knew more about me than anyone. Sitting and talking to him about personal things was no problem. Yet the thought of standing up and giving a short speech in front of him made me instantly nervous.

We weren't quite there yet, but it was looming in the near future.

First, Dr. Hulse had me bring in my recordings to play for him. This was the most anxiety-producing step yet, as I was to look at him as he listened to my speeches. It was a bit uncomfortable, but it went better than I'd expected.

I had been secretly hoping I could gather the

nerve to jump to the next step in this same session. I brought several favorite passages with me, in case I was ready. After we talked about the effect of the audio-tapes, I asked if I could give a speech. Dr. Hulse seemed pleased, and perhaps a bit surprised.

Well, it's now or never.

Dr. Hulse asked if I wanted him to face away from me at first. I declined his thoughtful offer, but decided I'd do the first speech seated. I gave my speech, trying to be as calm and clear as I could. I felt like I was on the verge of shaking and blushing, but I made it through.

It was now time for me to give a speech standing up. It was tougher than the seated speech, but I did it. Dr. Hulse asked if I wanted to do another. I did another. "Do another." I did another.

I gave five or six speeches, bam-bam-bam. It was somewhat difficult, but got a little easier each time. After all, this was the purpose of his plan: Expose me to my anxiety over and over to desensitize me to it.

Dr. Hulse said he didn't detect any of the things I felt—slight trembling and blushing, awkward swallowing. He said I did very well and pointed out that perhaps I was hyper-sensitive to these gestures, which probably went unnoticed by audience members. Again, it went better than I'd anticipated.

I was proud of what I'd done, but I didn't allow myself to get too big of a head. I still had a huge obstacle to face. It was like my team had just won the regular-season league championship, but we still had the playoffs and Super Bowl ahead of us.

Dr. Hulse and I agreed that my next challenge would be the real thing: Giving speeches to an actual audience. Toastmasters is something I have thought about doing for years. I didn't know much about the organization, just that they helped people become better public speakers. I researched Toastmasters on the Internet to see what I could find in my area. I printed out a list of local groups—eleven listings for Knoxville—and was pleased to find one that met at a church two-tenths of a mile from my apartment! This particular group held meetings on Thursday evenings from 6:30 to 7:30 p.m., which I could make on the way home from work. Everything was falling into place.

After my work with Dr. Hulse, I felt like it was time: I was as ready as I'd ever be. *I can do this...It will be so great to get over this fear...I'm sure it will be a compassionate group of people ready to welcome me and help me succeed....*

Thursday evening came around and I pulled into the church parking lot and saw a mass of people and about thirty cars. *What the hell have I gotten myself into*!? But I made myself go in to see what was going on.

They were there for a fish fry. *Whew.*

That evening, I learned that this particular club was small (which is just fine for me for the time being). When asked what brought me to Toastmasters, I confessed that I've had a fear of public speaking for a long time that I'm finally trying to get over. I breathed easier when the group leader acknowledged that about 90% of the people that come to their group do so for the same reason. I found this comforting: They've been in my shoes and will likely sympathize.

The purpose of Toastmasters is to help people develop better speaking, listening and thinking skills. Its mission is "to provide a mutually supportive and positive learning environment in which every individual member has the opportunity to develop oral communication and leadership skills, which in turn foster self-confidence and personal growth."

The first track of Toastmasters—"Competent Communication"—is a series of ten speeches. The first speech is called the "Ice Breaker," in which you tell the club about yourself. For each speech thereafter, the individual is free to talk about anything he/she wants. The Toastmasters manual serves as a guide to help members write their speech in an organized manner and improve each time.

At the time of this writing, I have completed the first three speeches and am preparing for my fourth. I have found my club to be very supportive: We genuinely want to see one another succeed. Every speech is evaluated to discuss what we did right and what we can improve on.

I have never really understood the origin of my problems, because I have always been well-liked and people seem to enjoy being around me. I've had my share of attention from the opposite sex, but it was never enough; a healthy self-esteem does not come from outside oneself. Shirley Trickett sums it up nicely in *Anxiety & Depression: A Natural Approach*:

> No matter how successful you may be in the present, or how many people tell you what a wonderful person you are, if you suffer from low self-esteem and are pushing around a wheelbarrow full of negative feelings about yourself, you are going to stay depressed.

With the help of Toastmasters, I am gaining self-confidence one speech at a time. It has been a challenge for sure, but you are free to go at your own pace. As my therapist taught me, the idea is repeated exposure: the more you face the fear, the more it diminishes. Each speech gets slightly easier. My goal is to get confident giving speeches and then wean myself off meds altogether.

I can't wait to finally put this fear behind me!

In addition to social anxiety, another issue that has plagued me is anxiety itself, often called "generalized anxiety disorder." The Mayo Clinic points out that anxiety is normal and often a good thing, unless it causes one to feel nervous without reason or if it disrupts your daily life: "Generalized anxiety disorder causes excessive or unrealistic anxiety and worry—well beyond what's appropriate for a situation."

For as long as I can remember, I have been a perfectionist and chronic worrier. For whatever reason, I obsessed over my to-do list and pushed myself far too hard. It was rare that I would slow down enough to truly enjoy anything fully.

Let me give you an example of how this has worked in my life. I have always loved to read. For most people, reading is one of the most relaxing things you can do. But for me, even reading became a source of anxiety. While reading, I would constantly worry about finishing a book: *How many pages do I have left? 50 pages, but only 42 if you take out the blank pages in between chapters* [yes, I would actually count]. *Ok, when I finish this book, then I will have* [counting] *1, 2, 3...12 more to read. I'll read the shortest one first to get that out-of-the-way....*

It was never-ending; instead of taking pleasure in the book I was reading, I rushed through it in order to be done and immediately start another book. That's how my mind worked. Reading a book went from being something I loved to do to something I had to get done, something to cross off my list.

I did not know how to relax. I didn't know how to slow down and appreciate things, only how to rush through them obsessively.

Life was an unending task of to-dos. From waking until I went to bed, it was a race to get things done. When I finally crashed for the night, I would fall asleep mentally listing everything I had to do the following day. After over-exerting myself every day, it's no wonder I felt lethargic and run-down all the time.

A typical weekday for me while in high school began with me forcing myself to get out of bed. Many mornings I would go down into the basement and do several drills to sharpen my basketball skills. Then I would study for my next test while eating breakfast. After school, I would make the fifteen-minute drive home to take a short nap, before returning to school for basketball practice. When I got home after practice, I would do homework until bedtime.

With such a rigorous regimen, I became so burnt-out that I decided to give up basketball my senior year. I wanted to have one year of high school free from the (mostly self-inflicted) stress and pressure. Sports, especially basketball, had been my main source of pleasure for so long, but had grown into something entirely disagreeable.

I didn't do much that wasn't in some way "productive." Still today, I might lounge by my apartment pool on occasion, but I'll also be reading and highlighting a book. Growing up, friends would ask me to play video games and I always thought it was such a huge waste of time. I would go home to do something I deemed worthwhile.

God love my parents, but this is the only way I knew. I rarely ever saw my parents sitting down and actually enjoying things. Even if they were watching TV or a movie, my dad would be grading papers or cleaning his electric razor and my mom would be clipping coupons.

I don't want to sound ungrateful; my parents are good people and have worked hard and sacrificed a lot for their family. I guess that's what you do when you are raising four kids on a teacher's salary. But the way I processed their example was to always be doing something productive. This ideal of the Puritan work ethic is ingrained in us in our society.

My problems with anxiety got so bad in college that I would constantly plan out what I had to do down to the last minute: *Okay, it will take me ten minutes to walk to the dining hall, fifteen minutes to eat, ten minutes back. Then, it will take fifteen minutes to shave and shower, which will leave me two hours to study before the party start.*

I was worrying my life away. I kept a to-do list in my pocket at all times and constantly checked off completed tasks. Throughout my school years, I never felt like "myself" unless I was on summer or Christmas break. The rest of the time I was a bundle of nerves, on and on, in a daily race against the clock. The end of final exams week was like shedding 100 pounds of weight from my shoulders.

Due to my anxiety (and social anxiety) problems, I was always on edge. I had trouble concentrating and had bouts of irritable bowel syndrome. As the Mayo Clinic says, "Many people with generalized anxiety disorder can't recall when they last felt relaxed or at ease."

I recall the strength coach checking my body-fat percentage in high school. After feeling how tense I was, he told me to relax so he could get a measurement. I told him I was as loose as I could get. Three times he asked me to release my tension and I tried to, but my body was always like that. That's just how I was and I hadn't even seen it as abnormal.

To combat my anxieties, I used alcohol to self-medicate. I drank far too much, far too often, for far too long. I thought the only use for a six-pack of beer was to add it to a twelve-pack. I have never been one to do anything half-way.

One night during my junior year of college, I was talking with a friend over several beers. He observed that everything I did was to the extreme, whether it be partying, playing sports or studying. I immediately knew he was correct, but the idea had never crossed my mind. I didn't know anything different. I assumed everyone was like me.

Alcohol did two key things for me: It enabled me to relax and it gave me more self-confidence. When I drank, I could stop obsessively worrying about what I had to get done or what others were thinking of me. I was laid back and care-free. I hated being tense and stressed all the time; this was my release, my magic elixir.

But I knew it was a temporary fix and not a good, healthy remedy.

If it weren't for meditation and therapy, I'd still be this way. I would be wracked with ulcers and on track to have a heart-attack by age 35. Even meditation was simply something else to get through at the beginning. Once my twenty minutes were up, BANG: I was off and running to get my next task done. I will talk more about meditation later, but one of the best things it has done for me was allow me to relax my overactive mind and body.

Meditation, yoga and therapy have become my support, albeit a much healthier, effective approach. This "holy triumvirate" has helped my anxiety problems immensely. It is still a challenge for me at times to slow down and relax after years of obsessive go-go-go (even now, if I am on the phone I begin pacing around like a squirrel on crack).

I am finally learning to relax without alcohol. I have cut back on drinking a great deal. I still like to have some beers with friends from time to time, but I am learning moderation instead of excess. Drinking has become more of an afterthought and less of the main focus. I do not need it as a crutch any longer.

Early on in my therapy, my therapist asked me what I wanted to do that evening. I replied that I was going to the gym and then to the grocery. He said that was what I felt I had to get done, but what did I want to do? I thought for awhile, but I had no clue. It was a foreign idea to me.

I always felt like if I got everything done today, then I could finally relax and enjoy tomorrow. But—you guessed it—there would inevitably be more to do the next day, and the cycle would start all over again. It was as if I were always saving for a rainy day, but missing all the sunny days in the meantime.

I am convinced that my long-time back pain was caused by my chronic anxiety problems. For years I held all my stress in my lower back. I was always on guard, far too tightly wound, and it was exhausting. My mental problems manifested themselves physically. The worse one was, the worse the other; they fed off each other.

On stressful days my back still starts throbbing, telling me to ease up. It took me far too long, but I am finally learning to listen to the wisdom of my body. I am slowing down and not pushing myself so hard.

I have come a long way with my anxiety problems. I am much more relaxed and try to do far less than I used to. For God's sake, I used to sneak in some reading during TV commercials and in my car at red lights!

Midwest Center for Stress & Anxiety CEO Lucinda Bassett has said, "My life, once filled with anxiety and depression, was once **endured** rather than lived" (emphasis in the original). The same was true for me. But as I said earlier, I am now starting to see my life as a blessing, an exciting adventure. Life is not meant to be an everyday struggle. I owe it to myself to slow down and enjoy life. I denied myself that pleasure for far too long.

Keep Fighting

At the urgings of my doctors, I tried a variety of prescription meds for both my social anxiety and anxiety problems (I consider them two different issues, though they often conspire together). I took several anti-depressants. But I never liked taking meds that I saw as simply treating the symptoms and not combating the underlying problems themselves.

Some of the drugs didn't help at all and some seemed to help for a few weeks and then it felt like I was taking nothing. And nearly all had side effects, from sexual dysfunction and extreme jitters to loss of energy. And let's not forget how expensive these meds can be: The big pharmaceutical companies are making a killing keeping us popping pills by the handful.

Don't get me wrong: Western medicine definitely has its place and has done wonders for countless people. But it also has its limitations. I have not had much luck with traditional health-care in this country. I have tried dozens of prescribed medications and often felt worse when I was on them. It was only after I started meditating and doing yoga, incorporated more positive thinking and getting on purpose (writing)—*as well as getting off most of my meds*—that I finally started feeling somewhat better.

Western medicine is stubborn and closed-minded. It fails to recognize the whole-person: the mind, body and spirit. All too often American doctors simply hand patients pills that do little more than treat symptoms, as opposed to getting to the root of the issue itself. When the magic chemicals do not work, they have nothing to say but, "This is just something you are going to have to live with."

Where does that leave people in my position, except feeling like a hopeless victim with a lifetime of suffering ahead? Luckily, I refused to accept the diagnoses and kept searching for a remedy. They might have given up on a pain-free, healthy life for me, but I have not.

I recall an interaction with the first rheumatologist I saw for my back problems. We had tried a few medications, but no good had come from them. My doctor said my next option was to try another medication, six pills every day. I expressed to him my concern about not treating the actual problem itself and taking so many pills, possibly for the rest of my life.

Visibly angry and almost yelling at me, he said:

"It's up to you. Are you going to take them or not?" I told him I would try a different route. (Ironically, I was asked to fill out an evaluation of my visit and I told them bluntly it had been the worst experience I had ever had with a doctor and that he was the least caring and most arrogant doctor I'd ever encountered in my life.)

At the opposite end of the spectrum, Dr. Andrew Weil says in *8 Weeks to Optimum Health*, "The most limiting omission in conventional medicine today is *the absence of the concept that the body can repair itself*" (emphasis in the original). A pioneer in integrative medicine, Dr. Weil recommends practicing yoga and meditation and maintaining a healthy organic diet. He favors natural remedies over the common Western chemical way. He is wary of the dangers of powerful, toxic chemicals and their effects on our minds and bodies.

I wholeheartedly agree with Dr. Weil that we need to address the whole picture. Body and mind are intricately linked. He says: "The simple and—I think—self-evident ideas that *the body can heal itself if given a chance*, that *it wants to be healthy*, and that *the tremendous healing power of nature is always there* to help are missing from contemporary medical research, teaching, and practice" (emphasis in the original).

I have continued my battle to find a cure for my

chronic pain and fatigue. Further testing at the sleep center found that sleep apnea was only one of my sleep disorders: I'm also narcoleptic. I was monitored at the sleep center for a series of four naps, each spread two hours apart, and fell asleep every time, which didn't surprise me a bit. (I was told that falling asleep once was normal, twice worrisome and four times astounding!)

The Mayo Clinic defines narcolepsy as "a chronic sleep disorder characterized by overwhelming daytime drowsiness and sudden attacks of sleep." Apparently my brain skips over the restful stage of sleep, leaving me exhausted each morning.

At any point of the day, I am confident I could fall asleep if given the chance to close my eyes for a few minutes. I have fallen asleep in an MRI machine twice, despite the loud clanging and machine gun-like noises. I can drink a cup of coffee or a five-hour energy drink and fall asleep a half-hour later.

I currently take a medication every night called Xyrem that helps with my sleep. It gets me to a more restful state that makes me not as tired during the day. It hasn't been a miracle cure that leaves me feeling refreshed every morning, but it has helped increase my daytime energy level much more than anything else I've tried.

I am not to the level of health that I want to be yet, but I am still fighting. I feel somewhat better now than I have in years. My mind and body are in a better place and still improving. I have made great strides in overcoming my struggles with anxiety, social anxiety and depression. Not surprisingly, my back pain has lessened as well.

*

"I learned how marvelously the mind can heal, given half a chance, and how patience and gentleness can put back together the pieces of a horribly shattered world."

–Kay Redfield Jamison, *An Unquiet Mind*

*

I once told my former primary physician that I suspected all of my health issues were rooted in some kind of nerve problem. He said, "The fact that you haven't jumped off a tall building by now tells me you have pretty good nerves." Though I never seriously considered suicide, I don't think he had a clue I'd thought about it a hundred times.

Alone once again when Mary left for Ireland, I instinctively knew I had to throw myself into my recovery: A lot of time alone for meditation and self-reflection, leaning on loved ones when I needed to and letting therapy do its work. I was finally forced to face my demons.

I still live a paycheck-to-paycheck existence, barely scraping by at under $23k a year. But I believe I am doing a meaningful job and helping others at Habitat. I often remind myself during these tough economic times that I am fortunate to have a job at all, and with much-needed medical benefits. I work with some good people for a great cause.

Lately I feel like I am on the verge of a new direction in my life. Perhaps I am getting closer to my intended path. For such a long time, I seemed to be sinking deeper into the darkness. Now I feel like I am rising toward the light.

Finally.

5

Count your blessings

"Once you replace negative thoughts
with positive ones,
you'll start having positive results."

–Willie Nelson, *The Tao of Willie*

Legendary singer-songwriter (and, in my opinion, sage) Willie Nelson said he had gotten so frustrated with his life at one point that he laid down in the middle of a busy street in Nashville, Tennessee, hoping a car would run over him. But none did. Since that experience, he made some changes and has done quite well, to say the least.

What stuck with me from Willie's experience was that when he started counting his blessings—instead of everything wrong in his life—his whole life changed. Ever since I read about his positive attitude, I have made an effort to give thanks for what I have, not focus on what I feel is lacking.

It hasn't always been easy. When you are often in pain and tired—in addition to struggling with anxiety,

social anxiety and depression—this can prove difficult. As my primary physician wisely said, "If you are
walking in the woods with a rock in your shoe, it's
kind of hard to enjoy the trees."

When I first started attempting Willie's strategy, I
would sabotage myself: *I am thankful for my family
and friends. Well, I have a great family and friends,
but most of them live four hours away, and they're
busy with their own lives...I am thankful for my
health. Wait a second, who am I kidding? I struggle
every day. My health sucks...* And so on.

But when I really looked around—**and not just at
those who were in a better situation than me**—I
began to see that I am more blessed than most people on this planet. When I consider all the people
living in Third World countries, not to mention the
homeless in my own country, I am probably better
off than a large percentage of the people in the
world. Millions, if not billions, of people would
switch places with me in a second, given the chance.

I now count my blessings every day. An "attitude
of gratitude" is far more beneficial for your well-
being than being bitter and envious. I promise you
that.

I had tried to make gratitude a practice every
night before I fell asleep. However, due to my narcolepsy, I'd be asleep before I finished, *I am thankful
for....* So now I give thanks in the shower!

The speech differs every day, but it might go something like this: *I am extremely fortunate to have been born in a free country. I am free to do just about anything I want, which billions of people in the world cannot say. I am blessed to have a wonderful family that loves me unconditionally. I have several close friends that would help me any way they could. I am lucky during these tough economic times to have a job and even luckier to have medical benefits. I have shelter from the elements and enough clothes to stay warm. I've always had enough food to eat….*

6

Faith and God

After years of being bitter inside, I have made a big effort to rid myself of toxic feelings. I am the first to admit that I have been mad at God. Very mad. I have asked for help time and time again, but it always seemed to go unheard. How could God let me suffer so much?

I am 31 years old and single. Although my physical health has improved slightly, I am not much better off than when I started searching for a remedy more than eight years ago. And, mind you, the pain and fatigue began years before I started looking for relief.

I was not pain-free and energetic one day in my 20s. Not one single day. This made me frustrated and angry. Sure, a 60-year-old will have aches and pains, I reasoned, but an active 20-year-old? It seemed extremely unfair to me and I blamed God.

But it wasn't only me that I was concerned with. I looked around me and saw people suffering everywhere. I saw homeless people on the street, others working two and three jobs barely getting by and families devastated by the death of loved ones serving our country. I saw people treating each other terribly.

On and on, so much pain and struggle. I was angry for what was going on both inside me and outside me. As Gandhi confessed long ago, "In the secret of my heart I am in perpetual quarrel with God that He should allow such things to go on."

But then I read a book that had a profound effect on my life: Rabbi Harold S. Kushner's *When Bad Things Happen to Good People*. Rabbi Kushner brings up an interesting argument: Perhaps God is not an all-powerful God that is always in control, as we are taught. If He were, then how could we explain all of the horrible things that happen to kind, decent people all the time?

Like Kushner, the unfairness didn't make sense to me. Neither of us wants to believe in a God that would permit such misery in the world. I tried to trust in an omnipotent and just God, but I couldn't when I looked at my life, not to mention Mary's. So I blamed God for all of the injustice I saw.

How dare He...?

But God could be a comfort to turn to during rough times and yet be unable to stop the bad things that happen. Kushner says, "The God I believe in does not send us the problem; He gives us the strength to cope with the problem." He points out that some bad things simply happen for no reason and therefore do not make sense to people, like me, who desperately search for an explanation for everything.

This intriguing notion caused a major shift in me. Perhaps God is not the source of all the difficulties in my life, in Mary's life, and in all those around me that I see struggling. Maybe God is not punishing us after all. I figure if it's okay for a religious man like Rabbi Kushner to believe this, then why not me?

I have a better relationship with God now. I have let go of much of the bitterness I held inside for so long. I try to be thankful every day for the many blessings in my life and I also spend a lot of time alone with God (my intuition, the Supreme Being...whatever other names you might choose) seeking guidance and simply listening. Striving to be more spiritual has made a difference in my life. I want to be a better person and deepen my connection with God.

Rabbi Kushner says it better than I:

> I believe in God. But I do not believe the
> same things about Him that I did years ago,
> when I was growing up or when I was a theo-
> logical student. I recognize His limitations. He
> is limited in what He can do by laws of nature
> and by the evolution of human nature and

human moral freedom. I no longer hold God responsible for illnesses, accidents, and natural disasters, because I realize that I gain little and I lose so much when I blame God for those things. I can worship a God who hates suffering but cannot eliminate it, more easily than I can worship a God who chooses to make children suffer and die, for whatever exalted reason...God does not cause our misfortunes. Some are caused by bad luck, some are caused by bad people, and some are simply an inevitable consequence of our being human and being mortal, living in a world of inflexible natural laws. The painful things that happen to us are not punishments for our misbehavior, nor are they in any way part of some grand design on God's part. Because the tragedy is not God's will, we need not feel hurt or betrayed by God when tragedy strikes. We can turn to Him for help in overcoming it, precisely because we can tell ourselves that God is as outraged by it as we are.

7

Meditation & Spirituality

"Within you there is a stillness
and a sanctuary
to which you can retreat at any time
and be yourself."

–Hermann Hesse, *Siddhartha*

*

"My life is primarily about meditation,
or quietly going within to discover
the invisible intelligence
and loving guidance that is
always available to me."

–Dr. Wayne Dyer, *Real Magic*

*

"When the student is ready,
the teacher will appear."
–ancient Zen proverb

When I was ready, the teacher that appeared was Dr. Wayne Dyer. As the Zen proverb says, I discovered his book *Real Magic* at the exact time I was receptive to it. Had I found it even six months earlier, I would have dismissed it almost immediately as some far-out, mystical BS. But when it entered my life, I was open-minded enough to give the book a chance.

After reading what Dr. Dyer had to say in *Real Magic*, I resolved to try meditation. Almost the next day, I stumbled upon a set of meditation cassettes, which described its benefits and included several guided meditations. I enjoyed the tapes so much that I began meditating regularly.

It was the best decision I have ever made.

Now I am far from a spiritual Master or enlightened being and there arc far more qualified people to discuss meditation, but I will give a simplified crash-course for those unfamiliar with it. Find a quiet place where you will be undisturbed. Sit cross-legged on the floor or upright in a chair with a straight spine. Close your eyes and concentrate on the inhalation and exhalation of your breath.

Try not to do too much in the beginning. Start with a short time-frame. Five minutes is enough. Simply sit, relax and observe your breath. Your mind may wander off in one hundred directions, but that is normal. Just come back to your breath. Over time you will be sidetracked less and less and you can sit for longer periods. If someone as scatter-brained as me can meditate for an hour or more at a time, I am confident anyone can!

Try to work up to twenty minutes twice a day, preferably at the same time each day. Remove any expectations and just be. You are not forcing, but allowing. Be still and retreat to that sanctuary within you that Hesse spoke about. It is a wonderful gift to give yourself and it may well be a life-changing practice for you, as it has been for me.

There are many different ways to meditate (counting your breaths, using a mantra and so on), but essentially you are trying to settle your mind and quiet the endless stream of thoughts cluttering your mind. Meditation is both simple—you are not actually doing anything, simply paying attention—and yet quite difficult. Westerners tend to have overactive minds that resist this "doing nothing." Our minds easily drift to what we "need to get done" or to what we "should be doing" instead. Steve Hagen explains in "Keep It Simple" (an article in the October 2007 *Yoga Journal*):

> Meditation often seems difficult because it runs contrary to how we've been trained throughout our lives. We've been brought up to get things done rather than just to be

present. In meditation, we stop clinging to that urge to do something that has been encouraged and bred in us for so long.

How many times have your best ideas come when you are taking a shower or driving alone in your car? That is because in those settings your mind is not as over-worked and over-stimulated as it normally is. Our minds are incomprehensibly amazing, yet mostly untapped because of the constant chatter on the surface keeping us distracted. I do not always like the person I become when I am stressed and rushed, but meditation puts you in a relaxed, peaceful mindset that has a soothing effect on you and those you come in contact with. The peacefulness and serenity that meditation creates cannot be adequately expressed with words; one must experience it firsthand.

We spend much of our lives ruminating over the past, though the past is over and done with. We get caught up in worry about the future, about what may or may not happen at some later time. But if our mind is constantly looking backward or forward, it cannot be here now. Meditation enables us to be fully present, in the present.

With sincerity, I believe meditation may well have saved my life: It kept me sane when I thought I might lose my mind and prevented me from having a nervous breakdown. It was my main support during the most tumultuous time of my life. Meditation also helped me tremendously with my anxiety problems.

Great for relieving tension and stress, meditation slows life down. It increases self-awareness and self-acceptance. Little things cease to bother you as much.

Many wonderful things seem to occur naturally when you are faithful to a regular meditation practice. Change didn't happen quickly, but in the eight years that I have been practicing, I can tell a real difference. Now, I often remain calm in situations where others are panicking. A sense of compassion and tolerance for others results and patience is greatly increased. I better appreciate Nature and the world around me, which I often missed in the rush of the rat race. "In meditation we cultivate a mind that *just sees* rather than a mind that is caught up in doing and seeking and achieving," Hagen explains (emphasis in the original).

Silence in our culture is highly underrated. As French scientist and philosopher Blaise Pascal said, "All man's miseries derive from not being able to sit quietly in a room alone."

My only regret with meditation and yoga is that I did not begin my practices years ago. I wholeheartedly believe both should be taught in schools and in the workplace. Students and workers would be far more creative, relaxed and focused. Therefore, they would be more productive. In this Age of Anxiety, where so many are over-worked, over-stressed and over-stimulated, we need yoga and meditation more than ever.

Meditation gives you access to divine guidance (many call this "intuition"). Dr. Dyer claims in *10 Secrets*: "It's the only vehicle I know of for making conscious contact with God."

In *What About the Big Stuff*, Richard Carlson explains further:

> Edgar Cayce said, 'Prayer is like talking to God; meditation is a way of listening to God.' That has been my experience exactly. When I meditate, I feel connected to God, as if I can hear the subtle whispers of insight and direction. It's very comforting and makes me feel as though I'm never alone.

I find this reassuring: You already possess everything you need inside you. All the answers, all the guidance you need is in you right now. We all have the potential to access it. It takes patience and discipline, but it is not something we have to search for outside of ourselves, as we are erroneously taught.

Much like Dr. Dyer's quote at the beginning of

this chapter, I find myself more and more wanting to spend prolonged time in silent meditation, instead of rushing around trying to get things done, as I did every day for so long. Meditation has helped me get my life more on purpose and has me doing what I feel I am on this Earth to do.

Meditation is a challenge for me due to my narcolepsy, as I fall asleep much of the time (while sitting up!). In fact, I often take a twenty minute power nap before I meditate, just so I don't nod off during my meditation. I am passionate about it and will continue to practice. As someone who was terribly over-anxious and always calculating, it was quite difficult to make myself do *nothing*, but I'm very glad I did. I have grown to love meditation and it has drastically enhanced my life in so many ways that I can't truly describe it.

8

Follow your heart
—or—
Getting on purpose

"Kahlil Gibran said, 'When you are born,
your work is placed in your heart.'
So, what is your work? Your purpose?
Are you living it out the way
your heart urges you to?"

–Dr. Wayne Dyer, *10 Secrets for Success
and Inner Peace*

*

"One thing I learned is that the mind,
rather than being the master,
should be the servant of the heart."

–Willie Nelson, *The Tao of Willie*

*

"There are risks and costs to a program of
action. But they are far less than the long
range risks and costs of comfortable inaction."

–John F. Kennedy

Whereas your right brain is your intuitive side that includes your feelings and knows what your purpose is, your left brain is always thinking logically and analyzing. Left brain tries to hush the guiding voices of right brain by refusing to take risks and fearing failure. As I have shown, I have been very left brain-heavy.

In *10 Secrets for Success and Inner Peace*, Dr. Dyer points out that listening only to the left side makes you "a commuter—getting up every morning going with the crowd, doing that job that brings in the money and pays the bills; and getting up the next morning and doing it all over again." A slave to my left brain, I have been a "commuter" for years. And if I don't do something different, I will remain one.

That little voice from the right brain never goes away; it is always there trying to get your attention.

I strongly believe we were all put here for a specific reason, to be aligned with our purpose. We were not meant to work ourselves to death, to live stressful, ultimately meaningless lives. To break our backs just to get by. Happiness is our birthright, is it not?

I don't want to wake up tomorrow and be 65 and full of regrets. I want to live-learn-laugh-love, to give and to grow, to travel and see the world, not simply "commute" in a suffocating kind of existence. Nearly every job I've ever had was just for making a living, but that kind of life is not fully alive to me. I agree with Bob Dylan: "He not busy being born is busy dying."

This struggle to make ends meet is certainly not conducive to creativity. I am tired of living in pain and being stuck. There's got to be more to life than struggle and disappointment. "You'll most likely always know when you're off purpose because of your thoughts of frustration," declares Dr. Dyer in *10 Secrets*.

I've been spinning my tires going nowhere because I have been off purpose. I've used logic to stifle what my heart has been telling me. My mind, heart and health (or lack-there-of) has been trying to advise me, but I wasn't listening.

Writing has always been part of my life. The need to write has been in me as long as I can remember and has been screaming to get out. I find it significant that I've often been bored and unchallenged at various jobs, back aching and glancing at the clock every five minutes. Yet once I am home, I can write effortlessly and pain-free for hours while time flies by unnoticed.

Writing this memoir is me getting on purpose. I am following my heart. I'm giving it a shot because I don't want to have regrets years from now. I am pursuing my purpose, wherever it may lead. "Regrets are usually greater for risks avoided than for those taken—even ones taken and lost," says Ralph Keyes in *The Courage to Write*.

I have no real training to be a writer per se, save a few high school and college English classes and a couple of weekend writing seminars. I resisted writing for a long time because I did not feel that I had any noteworthy experiences to write about, such as serving in an exotic location for the Peace Corps or spending several weeks road-tripping around the country (the latter a life-long dream of mine...my second book?).

But this memoir about healing kept pestering me, begging me to write it. In *On Writing*, Stephen King says, "If God gives you something you can do, why in God's name wouldn't you do it?"

I don't want to be in the same spot twenty years from now that I am in today. As Tony Robbins said, "If you do what you've always done, you'll get what you've always gotten."

I finally realized that it was up to me. I've been living a life of "comfortable inaction," to borrow from

JFK's quote at the beginning of this chapter: Never taking any chances or leaving my comfort zone. "Commuting" forty hours a week like so many other frustrated people.

I have spent a lot of much-needed time healing. I am determined to continue to turn things around in my life. There is so much I want to see and do. There is a whole world out there; I want to experience it...and I want to write about it!

-9-
Be gentle with yourself

"But pain does not represent God's
punishing us.
It represents nature's way of
warning good and bad people alike that
something is wrong."

*

"Our question will change from, 'why do
we have to feel pain?'
to 'what do we do with our pain so that it
becomes meaningful
and not just pointless empty suffering?'"

–Quotes from Rabbi Kushner,
When Bad Things Happen to Good People

My chronic physical pain was my body trying to tell me something; I just wasn't listening. I was doing too much and was on the wrong path. I was not being punished by God, as Rabbi Kushner pointed out, I was being prodded to change my ways.

For so long, I fought desperately, doing everything I could think of to finally feel better. It wasn't for lack of effort. But I had to learn to stop obsessively doing and begin to start being.

For example, the first time my thoughts raced out of control (the second being in my car on the highway) was not a stressful day at work, but an off day. As usual, I was running around like mad trying to get everything done, to make everything perfect. I learned the hard way, however, "perfect" is impossible: There's always more to do.

With this kind of obsessive thinking and doing, it's no wonder my body has been tight and aching. Years of anxiety have taken their toll, but I am working on undoing the damage with meditation and yoga. And it's not all that bad that many of my yoga classmates are fit females in spandex!

I am allowing myself to enjoy life more. I see the futility—and the hazards to my health—of pushing so hard. In the past, I would think about going to a park on a beautiful day, but I would rarely go. I'd decide it was a waste of time in which I could be productive (*By the time I drive there and back, I will have wasted at least twenty minutes* ...God forbid!).

At one time, I could not answer my therapist when asked, "What do I want to do?" Now, I not only ask myself that question, I often let myself do what I want to do, as opposed to what I feel I have to do. I still get done what needs to be done, but I don't push myself so excessively to do it all right now. In fact, I am more productive because I'm not trying to do ten things at once; I am more calm and focused.

*

"Our life is frittered away by detail...
Simplicity, simplicity, simplicity!
I say, let our affairs be as two or three,
and not a hundred or a thousand...
Simplify, simplify."

–Henry David Thoreau, *Walden*

*

As I was busy being productive, the world was passing me by. I am determined to make up for lost time. I now allow myself to slow down and appreciate life more. I no longer always expect perfection; I am more patient and gentle with myself. I have made strides to improve myself mentally, physically and spiritually and I feel I am headed in the right direction.

-10-
Don't be afraid
—or too stubborn—
to ask for help

I had been a listening ear for loved ones many times and I took pride in being there for support. Yet I was too proud to admit that I, too, needed others at times. I had been a good friend to them, but I had not allowed them to be good friends to me.

My mom taught me a valuable lesson about this. I told her once that I did not want to complain and burden friends and family with my problems. She said that people like to be asked for help; they want to lend a hand, but I had to let them.

One of the best things to come out of this whole ordeal is the unconditional love from family and friends. When I finally got up the courage to reach out, many people took my hand without hesitation. I received a lot of encouragement and good advice, but just knowing they cared deeply and backed me 100 percent was the most helpful.

I found it difficult to admit that I needed support, that I am a human being with frailties. I have had a lot of good times with my loved ones, but the crisis I experienced when Mary left was the first time I had turned to them en masse when things were not going well at all. But we all need each other in this difficult world. I know that now.

Life is much harder than I ever thought it would be. Everyone needs to be loved and understood. As His Holiness the Dalai Lama says in *Ethics for the New Millennium*, "Indeed, the more I see of the world, the clearer it becomes that no matter what our situation, whether we are rich or poor, educated or not, of one race, gender, religion or another, we all desire to be happy and avoid suffering."

As I learned, we cannot do this alone. If we could, what kind of life would that be?

I finally went to therapy, something I instinctively knew I needed for years (Truthfully, I've long thought everyone could benefit from therapy.) I have been working with a good therapist and he has helped me a great deal. I stopped running and I finally faced my repressed sadness, anger and fear.

It is a long, slow process. I spent years building walls around myself, but now I am tearing them down. It will take time and effort, but I am growing.

And it helps to realize I have many people to lean on...and it's okay to do so.

Forgiveness

I never stopped caring about Mary. I still pray for her and hope she is doing better than ever right now. I sincerely do.

But I was very hurt by how things ended with us. There were many lies and broken promises. Her leaving for Ireland—and not returning—left me shocked, lonely and depressed. I had to wait nearly three long weeks before I got any word from her. And in an e-mail, no less: Is that how you break the heart of someone that loved you and did everything they possibly could to help you?

Before Mary told me to move on, I still had hopes that we could recover from all that was plaguing us. I just wanted us to get back to those magical first months, when we were happy and in love. Then suddenly it was all over and I was farther down than ever before.

I may never have any answers about why this happened. So many questions remain.

But, as someone who has battled physical and emotional battles for many years now, I can't help

but feel some admiration for Mary. I know how difficult it is to hurt inside and out, to struggle every day.
I also realize her problems have been much more
severe than mine (and I have had all I can handle). I
know the tremendous frustration of trying so hard,
wanting so badly for some remedy, only to get let
down again and again.

So I feel an odd mixture of respect and awe for
Mary's amazing resiliency in the face of horrible
circumstances. The mental pain worsens the physical
pain and vice versa; it is a vicious, endless cycle.
They are so closely entwined that it is hard to tell
where one ends and the other begins; the two seem
to be evil, plotting twins working hand-in-hand.

As I said, Mary and I shared a strong bond of mutual
compassion for what the other was going through. I
can vividly recall times where I couldn't take any more
and would collapse next to her on the bed—where she
was often laid up with migraines and/or depression—
in tears of sadness, anger and desperation. We had no
idea what we could do to pull out of this hell. The only
thing we had was each other.

The first time I told Mary how much I respected
her for enduring so much for so long, she seemed
deeply touched. Like someone finally understood, at
least a little. Someone finally saw her not as a weak,
wounded animal to be pitied, but as a human being
that was forced to live with terrible conditions and

was doing the best she could. Frequent migraines and insomnia are both enough to deal with on their own, but to add an illness as devastating as manic depression to them is almost beyond belief.

I don't blame Mary for abandoning me. She was in a life-and-death struggle, and we both knew deep-down only she had the power to pull herself out of her hell. It was something she had to do on her own.

Had we stayed together, it may have killed us both. I see now it was a good thing that Mary ended things. Coming from an Irish-Catholic family myself, I relate to Matt Damon's character in the movie *The Departed*: "If we're not gonna make it, it's gotta be you that gets out, because I'm not capable. I'm fuck-ing Irish. I'll deal with something being wrong for the rest of my life." I had no intention of giving up on Mary.

Mary and I have exchanged a few e-mails since she went to Ireland, but we haven't talked on the phone or seen each other in person. As far as I know, she is still there. I replied to her first e-mail from Ireland and told her how hurt I was. I told her I would not give up on her and would continue to do everything I could. I told Mary that I loved her, but most of all I wanted her to be happy, even if it killed me (which it almost did).

That is probably the most loving thing I have ever told anyone.

Mary sent a few more sporadic e-mails in the next few months, as I tried to go on with my life. However, as I have said, I am stubborn and do not give up easily. The first e-mails told me she wasn't taking any meds—which both relieved and scared me—and was doing pretty well. Mary told me I was a great person and that causing me pain was the last thing she would ever want to do.

But she had no plans to ever return to Knoxville.

Another few months went by and Mary e-mailed again to tell me how sorry she was for how things turned out. She said she still loved me and thanked me for all that I was for her. Mary also said that if there was a God, then I was the closest thing to an angel that could ever be, which is one of the most touching things anyone has ever said to me.

But Mary also said she was only starting to grasp the depth of her problems. Again, I tried to tell her how special she was, that none of her emotional problems were her fault and that she was resilient beyond words. I told Mary that I'd always be there for her no matter what.

Another several weeks went by and Mary responded: She was getting by, don't worry...she had become too dependent on me and that wasn't fair...she could not put me through a lifetime of sadness...she wanted to call me many times, but then she would beg me to take her back...please move on...she'd be jealous but happy for me.

I do not know if we will ever cross paths again. Only time will tell. I am still healing, but I am now in a much better place mentally and emotionally: I have hope that I will meet my soul-mate someday, when it is meant to happen.

Mary will be a tough act to follow.

I forgive you, Mary, for any pain you caused me. I suppose you did the absolute best you could in extremely difficult circumstances. I realize you had to do whatever you could to save yourself and I don't blame you for this at all. You may well have saved me in the process. You still have a place in my heart and always will. I sincerely pray that you can overcome your demons and numerous difficulties. I am pulling for you.

As I have said many times: No one deserves to be happy more than you do. I greatly admire you for all you have endured; not many people could withstand half of what you've been through. I don't know that I could have.

A part of me will always love you. I hope you know I did the best I could. I wish you nothing but health and happiness.

PART V
LESSONS LEARNED...
AND TO PASS ON

A poor farmer's horse ran off into the country of the barbarians. All his neighbors offered their condolences, but his father said, "How do you know that this isn't good fortune?" After a few months the horse returned with a barbarian horse of excellent stock. All his neighbors offered their congratulations, but his father said, "How do you know that this isn't a disaster?" The two horses bred, and the family became rich in fine horses. The farmer's son spent much of his time riding them; one day he fell off and broke his hipbone. All his neighbors offered the farmer their condolences, but his father said, "How do you know that this isn't good fortune?" Another year passed, and the barbarians invaded the frontier. All the able-bodied young men were conscripted, and nine-tenths of them died in the war. Thus good fortune can be disaster and vice versa.

Who can tell how events will be trans-
formed?

–Story from the *Huai Nan Tzu*
(As quoted in Stephen Mitchell's New
English translation of the *Tao Te Ching*)

*

"I have been all things unholy;
if God can work through me,
he can work through anyone."

–St. Francis of Assisi

I love the story of the farmer above. What a great
message: It's pointless to get worked up over events
because we cannot foresee how they will play themselves out. When I am stressing over something—or
if I am overjoyed—I think about this passage and try
to come back to balance.

In *Eat, Pray, Love*, Elizabeth Gilbert says, "I
thought about one of my favorite Sufi poems, which
says that God long ago drew a circle in the sand ex-
actly around the spot where you are standing right
now." Throughout all of my struggles, I've told myself many times that, although I don't always understand it, I am right where I need to be. I've heard

many wise people say everything happens for a reason and I have reminded myself of this often.

I've often wondered why I have to be alone at this time in my life, but I see it now: I need this time to heal, to reflect and grow, as well as to write. Had I been in a relationship, I would not have had the opportunity to do these things.

I try not to be so quick to judge things that happen to me as "good or bad," "fair or unfair." It definitely didn't help me to think this way in the past!

In *The Power of Now*, Eckhart Tolle sums it up beautifully:

> Do you truly know what is positive and what is negative? Do you have the total picture? There have been many people for whom limitation, failure, loss, illness, or pain in whatever form turned out to be their greatest teacher. It taught them to let go of false self-images and superficial ego-dictated goals and desires. It gave them depth, humility, and compassion. It made them more *real* [emphasis in the original].
>
> Whenever anything negative happens to you, there is a deep lesson concealed within it, although you may not see it at the time. Even a brief illness or an accident can show

you what is real and unreal in your life, what ultimately matters and what doesn't.

When I read Tolle's words, I immediately thought: *Yes, that's it. That's what my struggles have given me: more* "depth, humility, and compassion." Life has been a struggle, but my trials helped me grow as a person. I learned what is real and what ultimately matters in life, as Tolle said. I gained a stronger love and appreciation for my family and friends and began trying to live a deeper, more spiritual life.

Often what we think is insurmountable is actually a blessing in disguise. For example, I was crushed when my girlfriend of almost six years decided to leave me. It sent me into a tailspin and I thought my world had ended.

But in retrospect, her leaving me was a good thing. Though I wouldn't admit it then, we were not right for each other. I tried desperately to make it work, but it wasn't meant to be. It was a fairy tale after all. It was painful, but she did me a favor by moving on.

The Dalai Lama nails it on the head in *Ethics for the New Millennium*: "The time of greatest gain in terms of wisdom and inner strength is often that of greatest difficulty." We learn and grow from our obstacles. What doesn't kill you truly makes you a stronger, better person.

The situation with Mary shoved me back several steps initially. It took me a long time to recover. But, as I slowly picked myself back up, I pushed past the point I was at before.

Dr. Wayne Dyer points out in *10 Secrets*:

> In a universe that's an intelligent system with a divine creative force supporting it, there simply can be no accidents. As tough as it is to acknowledge, you had to go through what you went through in order to get to where you are today, and the evidence is that you did. Every spiritual advance that you will make in your life will very likely be preceded by some kind of fall or seeming disaster. Those dark times, accidents, tough episodes, periods of impoverishment, illnesses, abuses, and broken dreams were all in order. They happened, so you can assume they *had* to and you can't *un*happen them [emphasis in the original].

My symptoms were there for years—physical and mental pain, financial difficulties and job frustration—telling me to make some changes. I struggled courageously, doing everything I could to "get better" or "find my way." I read all kinds of self-help books...swallowed my pride and sought therapy...

worked day after day at jobs I didn't like so that I could keep my head above water...threw myself 100 percent into relationships in which I got burnt...but I didn't give up. In truth, I was fighting bravely and looking everywhere I could for help.

But I wasn't looking in the right places: We are taught to look outside ourselves, but the answers are within us. "Everything you need for perfect balance and health is already within you," reminds Dr. Dyer in *Real Magic*.

If you are frustrated and feeling stuck, perhaps you are not on the right path. You deserve to be happy and do what you love.

You can only be at your full potential, your best self, when you are aligned with your purpose. And getting your life on purpose not only benefits you, it benefits those around you. Elizabeth Gilbert explains in *Eat, Pray, Love*:

> The search for contentment is, therefore, not merely a self-preserving and self-benefiting act, but also a generous gift to the world. Clearing out all your misery *gets you out of the way*. You cease being an obstacle, not only to yourself but to anyone else. Only then are you free to serve and enjoy other people [emphasis in the original].

Give meditation a chance. What have you got to lose? If you can't spare five minutes, twice a day, then you should *definitely* give it a try!

At the least, you will give yourself precious time to relax and unwind. However, I am confident you will receive far more benefits than these. I say again, choosing to mediate regularly is the best decision I've ever made.

Meditation has enabled me to deepen my connection with God. It helped me learn to be thankful for what I had and not get caught up in what was beyond my grasp. And it gave me a heart capable of forgiving people who had hurt me deeply in my life.

Listen to the wisdom inside you. There is so much that it can teach you. Whatever you call it—"God," "intuition," "the Supreme Being"—it is there to guide you. Let it. You are here for a reason.

What makes you happy? What makes time fly by for you? What "work" would you do for free if you could afford it?

You've got to follow your heart.

Perhaps it was my fate for my misfortunes to finally wake me up and get me on the correct path. Maybe I had to break down to my lowest point before I could build myself back up. In *Ethics for the New Millennium*, His Holiness the Dalai Lama says: "Unfortunate events, though potentially a source of anger and despair, have equal potential to be a source of spiritual growth. Whether or not this is the outcome depends on our response."

I urge you not to fight your battles alone. Don't be too stubborn—as I foolishly was—to let loved ones help you. Opening up to others shows that you respect them enough to ask for advice; you trust them enough to unveil your imperfections and to share your personal issues. In most cases, sharing will deepen your relationships.

It is okay to not be perfect. As we often see with our societal heroes, celebrities, politicians and athletes, no one is. Honestly, I don't think I'd like to be around someone that was perfect anyway.

Be gentle with yourself and learn to accept when you mess up. A wise person once said, "If you learn to laugh at yourself, you will be laughing all the time." I don't know about you, but the people I admire most are far from perfect. In fact, often their flaws—and their struggle to overcome them—endear them to us.

If you feel that you need therapy, don't be too proud to seek help. A lot of people out there—many who have been in your shoes—are ready and willing to show you the way.

As the saying goes, when you (the student) are ready, the teacher will appear [I want to point out here that the "teacher" does not necessarily have to be a human-in-the-flesh a la Mr. Miyagi. It could be a song, a book, a movie and so on.]. When I was finally ready to take on my biggest fear, Dr. Hulse was there to help me build my courage. Therapy has greatly enhanced my life and I look forward to my sessions and working to improve myself.

I believe many good things are in store for you and me. Things do have a way of working themselves out. Be patient and have faith. The Universe has a plan for us.

Get on purpose in your life and center on the things that truly matter. It's all about what you choose to focus on.

A greater power is in control. How messed up would this world be if we got everything we thought we needed? In the wise words of Willie Nelson, "Thank God we are not in control."

As for me, I am going to follow my own advice and see what happens. I am going to pursue my passion for writing with everything I have. In the introduction to his brilliant book *The Alchemist*, Paulo Coelho says:

> All I know is that…we all need to be aware of our personal calling. What is a personal calling? It is God's blessing, it is the path that God chose for you here on Earth. Whenever we do something that fills us with enthusiasm, we are following our legend. However,

we don't all have the courage to confront our own dream.

I am finding that courage. I look forward to the challenge. Coelho writes, "To realize one's destiny is a person's only real obligation."

I continue to confront and overcome my depression, anxiety and social anxiety issues, which limited me so much in the past. I am still optimistic that my physical health will continue to improve as my mental health does. I am less worried about being "cool" these days and more focused on becoming a better, kinder person. I am more grateful for everything that I have in my life and I look forward to deepening my spirituality.

While writing this memoir, my goal has become to move back to Cincinnati in the near future. I love Knoxville—the people, the lakes and mountains, the college football—but I want to be closer to my loved ones: my parents, siblings, nieces and nephews, as well as many dear friends from high school and college.

This time away from my hometown, approaching nine years now, was good for me; it made me realize how important friends and family are. But I have been gone long enough; it's time to go home. T.S. Eliot said, "We shall not cease from exploration—and at the end of all of our exploring will be to arrive where we started and know the place for the first time."

I have done quite a bit of healing. I am not claiming to be 100% where I want to be physically, mentally and spiritually, but I'm getting closer. I am on the right path.

As I've said, I spent years making my body tight with stress and worry, so it will take awhile to become loose and flexible. I am determined to overcome my rigidity, both physically and mentally. A new day is beginning and I am just waking up.

Faith over fear. I have no idea what is in store for me. I am okay with that. But I feel the next chapter is going to be amazing...

Acknowledgements

I have been very lucky to have help from so many wonderful people throughout this process. In many ways, I had no idea what I was doing and I appreciate the help and encouragement so much. I don't want to use the same old line *This book would not be possible without you*, but this book would not be possible without you.

To the three hundred or so literary agents who passed on this book, no hard feelings.

"Mommy" Sharon Cassada: Thank you for your keen edit. We've both been through some tough times and I appreciate having you to lean on. You've been a great friend!

Chris and Ann-Marie Torrence: For your support along the way, not to mention your tremendous kindness and friendship.

Dr. Lynn Nichols and the fantastic staff at Summit Sleep Services: For your courteous, professional efforts and for helping my narcolepsy a lot. Thanks for a job well done.

Joey Parker: For the great work you do. Thank you for taking the time to actually listen to what I was saying.

To my terrific yoga instructor, Pam Milner: Thank

you for sharing your knowledge and contagious enthusiasm of yoga with me and so many others.

Vidya Anderson, my dear meditation teacher: Thank you for your caring heart and for my personal mantra. The way you carry yourself may be your best instruction.

To my friends at Toastmasters: It is a pleasure to work with you all in such a supportive environment. I admire every one of you for striving to improve yourselves and facing your fears. Believe me, I know how tough it is! Thanks especially to Mr. Ken Roberts & Sandra Hall for your care and dedication.

To Araby Greene (book cover) and CJ Allan (formatting): Thanks so much for such quick, professional work turning my manuscript into an e-book. I'm glad I found you both, as that stuff is far beyond me.

Colleen Douglass: It's been a long time (10 years?) since you gave me that first blank notebook back at the Evans House at Miami U. I bet you thought I forgot, but I filled it up (and many more). Thank you for challenging me.

Julia Watts: For sharing your love of writing with me and many others. Thank you also for the generous offer to help with my query letter.

Tom Bird: Thank you for your valuable classes on writing and getting published. Add me to the long list of writers who have greatly benefitted from you.

Susan Frey: Though we'd never even met, you helped me several times as a favor to an old friend, my mom. Big thanks for your council and your many examples of unselfishness.

My friend in meditation and writing, Linda Weaver: you are my angel!! Thank you so much for your altruistic and invaluable advice, edits & encouragement. Your kindness is amazing!

Dr. Hulse: For everything you've done. You are great at what you do and I feel so blessed I was pointed to your office. I am forever in debt.

Aunt Jo/Uncle Don and Aunt Mari/"Uncle Godfather" Roger: Your unconditional love and generosity are much appreciated. I hope I can be half as good an example to my nieces and nephews as you all have been.

Christy, Laurie and Brian: I couldn't ask for better siblings. I admire each one of you.

Taylor, Morgan, Drew, Ryan, Katelyn, Amanda, Maddy and Henry: I am so proud of all of you and it is a pleasure to watch you all grow up. FYI, I may need some babysitters down the road a bit. Seriously, I hope you know you can always come to me. Remember to follow your heart!

Special thanks to all of my family and friends who stepped up with love and support when I needed it most. You all are too many to name here, which is a huge blessing in itself. I don't have the words...

Lastly, I'd like to thank my parents, who taught me to just do my best and that giving up was unacceptable.

With love and gratitude,

Keith

About the author

Keith Maginn was born and raised in Cincinnati, Ohio, the youngest of four kids. He attended Miami (Ohio) University as an Evans Scholar. After earning a Bachelor's degree in Sociology, Keith relocated to Knoxville, Tennessee, to work for AmeriCorps (a service organization like the Peace Corps, but within the U.S.). Since then, he has been working for Knoxville Habitat for Humanity.

The author loves playing and watching many sports, and also enjoys live music/concerts, writing, movies, meditation, yoga, reading and more.

Keith has been writing all his life, but *TURNING THIS THING AROUND* is his first attempt to be published. Keith is well qualified to write this book because he has lived it: this is a deeply personal self-help memoir. There are many self-help books written by psychiatrists, psychologists and so on, but the author typically has not personally lived through the hard times. No amount of training or second-hand experience can replace actually living the events on a daily basis.

Keith feels writing is his life's purpose and that he has a message to share that will help others. He hopes this will be his first book of many.

Connect with Keith on keithmaginn.com and https://twitter.com/Keith_Maginn

Made in the USA
Monee, IL
26 June 2025

20060096R00080